T0145124

RECALL PRIME NUMBERS EASIER

GRACE JOYNER

To order additional copies of this book, contact:
Xlibris
1-888-795-4274
www.Xlibris.com
Orders@Xlibris.com

ISBN: Softcover   978-1-7960-8164-0
       EBook   978-1-7960-8163-3

Print information available on the last page

Rev. date: 01/17/2020

RECALL PRIME NUMBERS EASIER

GRACE JOYNER

I studied the prime numbers and came up with a simple pattern for recalling them up to 100

Just remember these numbers:
2, 4, 2, 4, 2, 4,
6, 2, 6,
4, 2, 4,

then make a mental note of the number 53, after that,

Remember these numbers:
6, 2, 6, 4,
2, 6, 4, 6,
8

Prime Numbers to 100

1, 2, 3, 5, 7,
11, 13, 17, 19, 23,
29, 31, 37, 41, 43,
47, 53, 59, 61, 67,
71, 73, 79, 83, 89,
97

The numbers 1, 2, 3 are a given. For our purposes, we'll start at the number 5.

2, 4, 2, 4, 2, 4,

6, 2, 6,

4, 2, 4,

2 added to 5 = 7

4 added to 7 = 11

2 added to 11 = 13

4 added to 13 = 17

2 added to 17 = 19

4 added to 19 = 23

6 added to 23 = 29

2 added to 29 = 31

6 added to 31 = 37

4 added to 37 = 41

2 added to 41 = 43

4 added to 43 = 47

Make a mental note/remember the number 53.

6, 2, 6, 4,
2, 6, 4, 6,
8

6 added to 53 = 59
2 added to 59 = 61
6 added to 61 = 67
4 added to 67 = 71

2 added to 71 = 73
6 added to 73 = 79
4 added to 79 = 83
6 added to 83 = 89

8 added to 89 = 97

Just remember:

2, 4, 2, 4, 2, 4,

6, 2, 6,

4, 2, 4,

Then remember 53, starting
from 53, remember these:

6, 2, 6, 4,

2, 6, 4, 6,

8 (or remember the number 97)

Reader's Notes

Reader's Notes

Reader's Notes

Reader's Notes

Printed in the United States
By Bookmasters